Sun Ripened Fun Ideas

Volumes One & Two

Robert Wildwood

Cover Artwork by Jordan Sundberg
tincupdesignco.com

Published 2025 by Free Water Press
ISBN: 979-8-218-59050-5

for
Beatrix & Raymer
with Love from Pappa

If you found this book be assured it is not lost or forgotten. Many of these have been placed in public places for readers to enjoy. The book is now yours to read or put back down for someone else to find.

If you bought this book at your local independent bookstore, thank you for supporting a business that operates in a spirit of passion for community.

Please drop me a note:
RobertEarlWildwood@gmail.com
to share your experience finding this book
and any other thoughts. Thank you.
Love.

This book was written in a place called Misaabekong (the place of the giants) and Onigamiising (the place of the small portage), also known as Duluth, on ancestral and contemporary land of the indigenous Anishinaabe, Ojibwe, Chippewa, Dakota, Lakota, Cheyenne and people known by other names who still live and thrive here while protecting the living land as they have done for thousands of years.

We oppose the colonialism, white supremacy, and genocide that indigenous people have resisted on these lands for more than 500 years. With this statement we affirm native sovereignty and strive to respect indigenous people with our actions.

Sun Ripened Fun Ideas
Volume One

Table Of Contents / Volume One

Embrace Being Awake / 006

Prepare To Love / 014

Enjoy Our Body / 022

Know This Cycle / 034

Feel Truth Love Fire / 042

Embrace Being Awake

Splash Water

With cupped hands bring cold water to your face in the morning and wipe clean. Every spirituality knows the power of water in us. Splash water on your face using clean hands once, twice, three times. Now from the deep float up and surface, awake like born from the flow, welcome again, this is today. Thank you. Splash warm water on your face to transition from work to play, wash away old molecules, every moment holds the possibility of a new vision. Finger snap slap send signal through synapses light up the brain. Wash away the words of work stuck to your face, warm soapy water the spittle and grease returned to Earth towel dry skin touches fresh air brain lights up an almost forgotten idea oh yes now laughing out loud hoot and howl ready to give and receive love.

Wake As Water

Today i woke up as water
following gravity down through small cracks
it took a long time past soil layers worms rocks
into a creek going faster out to freshwater sea flowing
i enjoyed evaporating
following invitation of the sun and
leaving liquid behind fly as gas fun yet not grounding.
In a cloud of friendship we cooled dense dark
fell as rain on loved ones and liquid again
washed them clean listened to their laughter
as we understood the joy of cycles
would bring us here again
through every body alive
one at a time.

When Everything Is Here

Awake in the quiet energy of the storm wind strikes chime sounds chord over subtle flow rain water under iron disk the basement pipes flow are we floating awake thinking John Brown's rebellion multi national corporations some burnt to the ground the ones that survive will be stronger rush in to fill the void bad flow broken glass canning jar accident wet brown paper bag too much at the end of the day four inches of rain earthworms sun going down the young one finds worm after worm needing rescue moved off path to safety of grass the creek at flood stage our quiet wading pool where water relaxes on journey to Superior Sea where she wets her feet and watches crawdads and floaty strider bugs now a raging rapids guaranteed death pounding roar transformation extreme spectacle of spring so we all move closer to take photos and dip a toe in the wild get shoe wet testing boundaries feel flow interior to our body hearing call to observe then flowing to a following circle of friends strangers organizing unknown rebellion unknown even to ourselves to surprise everyone. In the background nagging voice says go back to sleep workday tomorrow capitalism calling needing our energy deep below a river of everything always sounding quiet flowing we do not have ears to hear i am still awake listening.

Embrace The Body

Born in this living skin amazing without perfection there is no other option a future of synthetic form transferable consciousness select a new body not possible today we live in the body alive as born and ever changing a body alive broken and healed remembering pain and trauma love and joy footnotes attached marked on genetic code a gene that precludes eating gluten a gene that began removing head hair at a young age a gene activated in puberty immune system inflammation on skin out break of psoriasis embrace this body the shape the color the smell embrace this body gifted this temple of self often desecrated wild youth and now so carefully tended asking what do you need today body i am chief executive officer outnumbered by bacteria my cells dancing with multitudes i see you We jiggling mass of many things and honor our struggle surviving our decisions embracing this fortunate body still walking still breathing.

Apply Pressure, No Peeking

The feeling of using your hand to apply pressure and stop bleeding on an injured person is very satisfying.

Recoiled from fountain of blood,
transformed quiet wound bed of calm yellow bubbly fat, yes you did that.

The feeling of using your hand to apply pressure and stop the bleeding in a wounded stranger
is a good feeling,

like we are one and there is reason to believe in us.
One world, many people, we are one.

Feeling Like Trees

Negative emotions as tools anger can show us what is wrong anger can help us be happy. In autumn deciduous trees pull green chlorophyll back into branches and trunk leaving only yellow pigment in leaves. During winter trees store these chemicals needed for their leaf solar panels safe inside wooden body for spring. Anger is a useful emotion people motivated by anger can achieve success anger is different than hate. Rigid thinking makes it hard to deal with problems. Being open minded and flexible makes us better problem solvers. A forest can act like a body of water, when it is too hot trees open stoma under their leaves to release water vapor and cool the environment of the forest.

Think About Connection To Home

Being transplanted is hard, it damages your roots. The tips of tree roots have structures that make decisions like neurons in the brain and can communicate then share food sugar with other trees and decide how much water to drink. Tree root tips make connections with fungi and we wonder what they talk about. Parent trees pass their knowledge on through epigenetic markers in their seeds to tree children. Tree children know how to grow in the soil their parents lived in and know about rainfall amounts and average temperatures. If the root tips are damaged or cut off communication becomes difficult, it is hard to repair, if the root tips are not touching other root tips there is no one to communicate with and the tree is alone. An isolated tree may only have a crow or squirrel for a friend. Communication is important isolated trees are vulnerable squirrels and crows can spread tree seeds planting thousands every year while caching them for food in the coming winter but maybe they know some of them will be forgotten and then grow to make more nuts as adult trees who are we to say what thoughts are thought in an unknowable mind. Saplings raised in a nursery given food and water never knowing scarcity, never knowing hunger or thirst, have a hard time when they are transplanted to the wild.

Prepare To Love

Destroy Them

"What's in your mouth!? Let mommy have it." eleven month old still experimenting with taste texture and found objects nothing tasty about a Bot Fly pupae. "What the fuck is this?" "Oh my god, he had that in his mouth?" Now we are both doing research online will our baby be okay having placed the pupae of a parasitic insect in his mouth things no one thinks to learn about before becoming a parent. A university extension expert advises: your baby is safe the fly stage lays eggs under the skin, not the pupae stage. Check your cats for wounds of larval stage infestation and if you find more pupae laying around: destroy them.

Consider Climbing The Slide

Adult control is illusion we think it's a one way ride children know better move beyond illogical boundaries yes it is customary to go down a slide the easy gravity fly children create new thrill at challenge yes it is fun to slide down it is also fun to climb up explore the unknown reach the top by transgressing rules prove possibilities in forbidden pathways. Who's playground is this.

Prepare for Never Ending Change

Daughter, are you ready? You slept between us and every night i would tell you a story the only way to soothe anxiety and invite sleep jack and the beanstalk but then we got bored and the story changed the giant's toilet broke and he had to poop by hanging his butt over the edge of the cloud and jack lived down below so endless amusement and you laughed so loud you requested that story every night until i regretted making it up but then your brother was born and everything changed now we had to be quiet all tucked in the king size bed and your brother in his little side car bed now our story time was in the other room and i read four books before bed but no more spoken story, laying in bed now just listening to your brother breathe while he slept and you respected his needs quiet as a mouse you played the part and when he woke up crying you put your sound dampening head phones on and lay back down to sleep. Accepting your role the best big sister. Loving him mad at him laughing at him you performing antics to make him laugh and he crawled over and put his head in your lap you said "Aawww he loves me!" Yes I think he does.

Stop & Listen

now is the time when your shoes fit into mine I saw you tuck your little bright colored slip-ons into my big dark colored slip-ons and they fit in there just right. Now is when we are that close. I was the stay at home parent the first few years now I am gone four days a week at work and i miss you, us, sometimes you are so angry when I get home demanding i answer questions is that just a four year old and learning emotional complexity, having a hard time adjusting to a little brother i try to go to where you are sit on the floor with both of you and hold your anger help your joy emerge the night ends with us reading together. This must be good we are doing. Keep asking angry questions i will keep listening as calm as i can feeling my silent breath moving in and out.

Nourish The Light Within

Practice pulling light in holding calming healing light practice pulling light in with each breath then sending light through hands through air through Earth to someone who needs it a point of light begins and grows until they become engulfed in radiance i practice this every time my children fall asleep where did this idea come from unknown just started doing because it felt like i should at best i really am transmitting healing calming energy light or maybe just affirming intentions for our lives and family. Connection. Visualize the reality we want. Manifesting joy in magical light.

Try Horizontal Parenting

Lay on the living room floor. My eight month old son cannot resist the poppa jungle gym climbing over me slapping laughing jumping up and down like a horse ride soon my four year old finds me too she was a baby once doing the same thing and forgot about it until she saw him and now they wrestle and giggle on top of me. i close my eyes and rest. Let the dirty dishes and laundry rot don't let anyone call you lazy when you spend time connecting with your kids.

Easy & Cheap Ideas For Raising Children

* Swaddle a newborn to comfort them. Wrap them in simple cotton cloth like a burrito, tight, holding their arms at their sides. They just spent 9 months in a cozy fetal position, to go from that to sticking your arms and legs out and not touching anything has gotta feel weird. Swaddling is instantly soothing to many

newborns. When a newborn is ready to experience the world without being swaddled they will let you know.
* Feeling tired? Lay down! Horizontal Parenting is a great way to connect with your kids while resting your entire body. Attachment parenting when your kids can attach to any part of your body, including the areas that are usually out of reach above their heads. Remove glasses & jewelry first. Tie back hair.
* Make a priority of nourishing your relationship with your parenting partner. A strong connection between parents will give the children a solid base of security. Our children are watching and listening to every interaction between us, what are we teaching them?
* Check in with your parenting partner once a week minimum. Communication gets hard you have to be intentional and schedule that shit. Make tea, eat cookies. Talk.
* Someone having a meltdown? Step outside with them or open a window and breath new air. If there are trees nearby they will be releasing chemicals called phytoncides that have been shown to promote wellness in humans. Feel your breath go in and out, notice a wider world around, contemplate perspective. Who am I. Yes. We remember.
* A bag of small frozen blueberries can be great for a teething toddler to chew on, cools and delights the mouth after a warm meal.

* Play! Try having fun with your kids. Nobody wants to listen to an authority figure. Try talking in the voice of a character and have fun with communication. Using a stuffed animal to talk to your kids might work better when they are angry at you and don't want to talk, a neutral third party. Play! Make life a game, include things that need to happen as part of the game. It's way more fun than trying to make the Command and Demand model of parenting work. Play!

*In all interactions with your children consider this: are you pushing them away, or pulling them closer?

Enjoy Our Body

Try Physical Therapy Before Drugs Or Surgery

Lower back pain torments many people. The causes are different for every person but for me i learned from a wise massage therapist that the Psoas muscles which connect our lower back bones to our hips and legs can become tight and will cause lower back pain. He taught me a step lunge and hamstring stretch which relax the Psoas. After just 5 minutes of doing these stretches the pain in my lower back dramatically lowers.

 At the point of pain experience when i was about to explore drugs or surgery to make the pain stop, i was gifted a simple and easy way to alleviate the pain. Stretching.

 This type of experience with health care has played out multiple times in my life. Sometimes going directly to a doctor skips the most knowledgeable healers with easy solutions and puts us on the road to endless interventions with drugs and surgery. Doctors can do amazing things sometimes, as a nurse i work with doctors every day, but for our health care we must be our own advocates. We must investigate our body and ask for help from many different healers to develop a view of what is our personal health truth. We have the power to know and sometimes heal our body.

Be Mindful Of What Happens When You Put Things In Your Body

Some intakes are obvious like when i ate a dozen crayons and pooped a rainbow but some effects are subtle like connecting being angry with the amount of caffeine intake. When we consume something every day why would we connect it to some specific result? Not until we consciously decide to regulate consumption will we notice changes. For years i suffered fatigue, brain fog, gastrointestinal upset and then one day 3 beers into a six pack on a camping trip i got real sick and my tent companion said "Maybe you are allergic to wheat gluten. You should get checked." Yes sometimes we need help to recognize a hard truth. i worked as a baker for years. i loved wheat. used to break open a loaf of bread and huff the aroma. Nobody wants to let go of something they love even when it's hurting them. That's what a real friend is for, to put their hand on our shoulder and say, "Let it go." Listen to your friends.

    Be mindful of what happens when you put things in your body. Working in long term care as a nurse i would come home and stress eat just to feel good and relax and distract from the day of work, then lay down immediately to sleep but this caused acid reflux from my stomach. A conscious decision to not eat two hours before laying down was hard to do but important for my health. Living with a long term partner made it necessary to coordinate this healthy timing of consumption. No more late dinners for me before laying down with the children to help get them to sleep, no acidic foods for dinner, no alcohol before bed. Being mindful of what happens when you put things in your body is a level of adult that i wish had been achieved sooner.

    Be aware of what goes into your eyes and ears, it adds up. Media advertisements are reprogramming your brain to have a desire to consume a product. Time spent watching shows or surfing the internet is programming your brain, our conscious mind will be overwhelmed by stimulus and you will find yourself spending money on things you never wanted before. Advertising exists because it works. Advertising works very well, it can be scientifically measured. Hit mute during commercials and speak your own dialog. Pay for ad-free, probably cheaper than what you might buy after being brainwashed.
Turn it off.

Focus Of A Living Room Should Not Be A Screen

Tucked in a corner a small quilt covers the obsidian colored flat screen receiver of signal and projector of visions. When the screen is off it is put away. A screen

is not the default focus of this room, our living does not center on what comes from the outside. Facing each other eye contact words exchanged hands touch bodies cuddle listening to each other hot chocolate tea and coffee we are deprogramming we are living.
Real friends and family bleed.
The average adult spends 10% of their lifetime watching a screen. You are what you do. I am 10% corporate programming. What could I do with that 10% instead. Deprogramming continues. Thinking of our children screen time is a crime against their future where is balance in this abundance of digital chaos. Cultivate a culture of mindfulness and sacred space and time where digital devices are forbidden watch us go extreme to protect our children at the circuit box a hand on the main breaker mysterious power outage we look for candles and read magic spells in the dark smiling into each others eyes.

Welcome A Stranger

We put a jumbo size little free library and a big bench next to it right by the sidewalk and have met many neighbors who stopped to look at the books and the flowers in the garden and the sky and made real neighborhood connections. Children come running up the hill from the bus stop to the little free library and look in it to see if there are any new treasures. Now i think any house we live at should have a public bench right there on the sidewalk just to invite people to slow down relax connect chill feel welcome on the land where they live. There is no trespassing here on the border of what has been established as public and private lands. This bench and tiny library are an invitation and a recognition that our hearts are big enough to share with strangers.

Listen When Intuition Speaks

Consider the unseen small things particulates in air affecting populations why everyone at the clinic has a systolic blood pressure 10mm Hg above their baseline after two days breathing smoke Canadian wildfires hearts working harder anecdotal not evidence based this nursing intuition speaks storm arrives at night drop in barometric pressure all the children wake up we are all awake and feel the pressure drop deep inside parental intuition speaks we are all living in the same environment who is doing a study on this We for example when the full moon illuminates intuition pulls us through doors and we stay out late hunting for pleasure gathering friends joining the party to share gifts release our suffering and celebrate being alive we need this connection to thrive.

Process The Emo Harvest

Here again another reaping of emo fruit. Mr. Rogers suggested we might harvest from the garden of our mind. What will i do, who to share these vegetables of anger with, a small brown bag I will give to someone who cares, my neighbor Bob maybe, a small jar of sweetened love but who wants these filthy rotten tomatoes of hopelessness and my burnt cucumbers of anxiety. Face the compost bin and one by one let them go even the fallen cornstalks of curiosity our dream of October corn maze now a flattened crop circle mystery. Pull a blanket over my eyes rest now, next year, next year.

Make A Big To-Do List

~~emerge~~
~~survive~~
~~get big~~
~~do things~~
~~get smart~~
~~kiss~~
~~travel~~
~~party~~
~~make friends~~
~~avoid evil~~
~~get therapy~~
~~gain skills~~
~~produce~~

~~create~~
~~move into love~~
~~reproduce~~
~~nurture family~~
~~be happy~~
stay happy
maintain friendships
maintain family
become wise
share knowledge
uplift people
share love
reach out
do good
be courageous
defeat evil
let go
invent
create
be truth
recreate
be love
inspire
let go again
give
die

Work Part Time Live A Decade Behind

Economic adjustment, personal priorities, economic time travel, freedom from compulsory consumption. Less time working equals more freedom. Less money means more budget. Purchase only out-dated merchandise, ten year old fashion half price or free. A decade ago people were excited about this stuff the latest and greatest. We too can be excited about the old and obsolete run your mind back ten years imagine the excitement. Never buy expensive new products of today they will be old and discarded in a decade. Reset the clock and go part time now (the exception is food and don't be fooled most of what they sell is a scam) Walk the woods breathe the magic you have time when desires are not manufactured to maximize profit. Love of old, love needle and thread the very latest fashion at your fingertips. New car never never never. Drive to the gym no simply walk if you can walk humble truth as blood and lymph flow lucky we and fortune blessed thinking we are different and how are we strong to resist advertising the desires planted like weeds by forces capital holding us disciples of products captured in catalogs. Intentions return to manufacturing our happiness with no fee reality.

Talk With Your Amygdala

Amygdala reacts, consciousness replies: No I've got this I am still in control we do not need to fight flee or freeze right now it's a lot to explain my amygdala you guardian of me see right now we are experiencing what is called a trigger it's a situation that is like a similar situation we experienced in the past but this is not the same situation this is different and we can do this another way. Amygdala, i am shutting down the fight flight freeze response that is not helpful now thank you for offering. i want our children to grow up in a world of calm, not curses.

Practice Calm Curiosity

Greet unexpected anxious moments in a new way: with calm curiosity. Responding with instant anger and harsh words has never resulted in joy. Yes try something new, even take a pill if you need to, imagine we could enjoy every moment alive if we were ready to meet it with calm curiosity. Why is this person acting this way, why are they saying these things, i can feel that it's upsetting to me but this person is not in control of my emotions. Recognizing my emotional response i embrace my response. What if we could enjoy every moment alive if we were ready to meet it with calm curiosity. Imagine.

Accept The Challenge Of Communication

The struggle to connect is not fun sometimes painful then exciting to see light emerge. A family is communication, all growing changing breathing crying laughing wrapped in home. The end result of communication is fun. Communication gives the unknown a form, now the unknown has a name. You can say hello to it. The unknown is upsetting scary confusing. False perceptions prevent communication of hidden truths, water for thirsty water to cool anxiety extinguish hate fire. Communication is our challenge at home and on Earth, we have a lot of talking and not enough listening.

Write Something Fun

i think about death a lot, not in a way like being afraid or obsessed but curious and always in comparison because i have never been dead so i have no reference. Look there is a guy just walking around one hundred years old seems fine but he will be dead soon, and there is a young guy riding a scooter reckless in the street at night no lights wearing sunglasses no helmet he could be dead in seconds or live to a hundred my grandfather lived to a hundred and i am halfway there now but i am not my grandfather so what goes on deep in my body gene expressions turned on turned off cells collaborating what are they building in there my young children need me alive my partner too so tell myself hey we need to last a long time so what do you need more sleep less stress okay that sounds good conscious mind listening to body quietly talking and miracles of modern health care longevity of life only getting longer watching an old guy gray hair using a walker battling high wind and holding helium balloons don't loose the balloons i am rooting for him from safe inside glass lobby okay he did it got the balloons inside the car i almost went to go help it could have been anyone it could have been me he looked a little old and i thought about death but then he shoved the walker in the car and walked away.

Know This Cycle

End The Anthropocene

What is human. Can human survive the age of human, adapt to our destructive domination and rejoin the cycle of life on Earth. The word human from Latin: humus = Earth. Live and die and let everything live and die without micromanaging nobody likes a micromanager going in to clean up the forest with the noble intention of making it healthy like somehow forests were ill during the millions of years before we arrived to take care of them. Fake science funded by multinational corporations to gather money for the short lived Anthropocene party i usually love a party but this one needs to be shut down before the house catches fire we do not have a big enough fire truck y'all are fucking up start pumping the brakes I sold my car I'm walking to work my gas is oatmeal it goes in the stomach cheap and no added greenhouse gas emission in the winter wear more clothes easy are you with me tonight do you feel the fire stand up start counting we don't need everyone on board just enough people to steer the ship away from the whirlpool.

We The Weed Are Also The Gardener

Success is our pathogenesis. Apex predator nothing to hunt but ourselves now spread across planet every summer like creeper vine or knot weed invasive shading out indigenous life demanding adaptation assimilation or extinction leaving behind empty husks of shopping malls and toxic wood stick nests confusing concrete foundations footprint long lasting when somewhere long ago in East Africa we stood up and wandered away no more trees stood up and looked down on the four legged ones running chasing running into the open unknown horizon foot follow foot modern marathon we are today here still running. What now. A weed is whatever you don't want growing in your garden.

Behold A New Day

Corporate builders never get it right always trying to force people into their structured vision, always trying to get that patch of grass to grow between sidewalks that becomes trampled into hard dirt where people insist on walking because it is a short cut and people are not robots who walk and make turns at perfectly precise right angles we wander we explore we trespass we disobey because natural selection has favored this trait try to wall us in we will find a way out dig a hole underneath or around find a way an unlocked door climb to the top and slide down. The carpet of humanity that covers Earth was not born into quiet contentment we desire to climb the very tallest building or spend our lives building machines to take us to another planet and it makes sense it is a pathology if we do not roam and spread out we will consume each other so there on top of a skyscraper a brave heart takes a selfie and smiles knowing nobody can touch them at the top of gravity hierarchy a photograph documents the unique achievement that pathological capitalism demands colonize the peak of every building and mountain plant your flag or acquiesce to performing a support role for the climbers and for humanity we wonder what is next. Does the end stage lead to a new beginning or a new day without us.

Enjoy Primitive Recreation

Walk into a dark bathroom and wait for the light to come on in darkness find the doorknob and lock it still waiting this is not a smart bathroom we begin to realize hand reaches out for where we remember the switch is. New season transitional technology society in modern workplace we hardly use light switches dark rooms illuminate as we enter like gods touchless world future season historically searching for matches in the dark before that stepping out into moonlight returning digestion results directly to soil contemplating like skunks and squirrels we call this camping but we could call it time travel, exploration of a past or future where plumbing and toilet paper are gone.

Get Ready To Surf The Atlantic Meridional Overturning Current

How many of us on Earth know this engine of life
A.M.O.C. the Atlantic Meridional Overturning
Current, mover of heat from tropics to the north
redistributor of thermal wealth unseen under ocean
just doing what it does until one day it doesn't. If this
current collapses extreme weather will get extreme,
temperature fluctuations 30 degrees Fahrenheit
different than usual. Mass crop failure and famine
worldwide infrastructure failure war all in the future

yes yes look how fast those children grow, can you believe it, and suddenly the future is here.

Motivational Mantra

Our children need a planet that works. Go.

We Already Did This

We have damaged and then healed the Earth before. The atmospheric ozone was being depleted by chlorofluorocarbons we were putting in the air so people rallied and compelled governments and business to stop and they did and the hole in the ozone closed. We problem solved.

Catastrophic climate change can be stopped the same way. We have done this before. We have damaged and then healed the Earth. The main problem now is the people who are making money from processes that put greenhouse gases into the atmosphere are much more powerful than the chlorofluorocarbon industry was back then. The capitalists who do not care about the future have found a way to shut us up and pretend that there is nothing to see behind the curtain. We know their names.

We have healed the Earth our home and we can heal our home again. What year will it be that the future looks back and remembers as the time when the balance shifted when eyes opened when we took a deep breath when we chose to love the world more than money and power. We can do it this year, but desire is not magic. Action. We are many people. We are one.

Beware The Architects Of Moral Panic

Manipulating vulnerable minds for personal gain responsible for murder in large numbers the architects of moral panic turning out lights and making monsters in the dark using fear of the unknown to control populations, shifting power from the many to the few. Every day we turn on and let the voices in, imagining we are using free will to choose, but is it all the same channel? Every day we have the opportunity to learn. Who is our teacher and who is paying them to teach us? What are we being taught?

Love The World

Consumption contemplation our fork in the world tasty meats from factory farms and our lungs connected to the respiration of ancient forests and massive buildings full of people manufacturing our demise. We only see the top of the iceberg but it may soon be melted and we looking up from underwater adapting to swim. How can the truth survive the spin of those who profit from lies. Do your best do what you can long game get as far as we can teach the dream to a new generation. Keep your head above water.

Encourage A Long Overdue Reckoning On Capitalism

Keep watering the good life growing keep nourishing the roots of love. The foundations of exploitation are cracking the truth is leaking out a flood of fire is coming remove all combustibles from your community store them safely circle your circles gather your light and start the music prepare for struggle prepare for freedom prepare for backlash those who desire control at any cost will not listen to love or truth, they must face our courage and feel our fire. We must hold those who do harm accountable.

Whatever political party is currently in power you still have the rich getting richer and the poor getting poorer. No more blaming politicians we know they all serve the same master, the global matrix that is responsible for the oppression of humanity: it is time to put Capitalism on the ballot.

Feel Truth Love Fire

Listen To The Quiet

In darkness my eyes opened body vibrating resonating hum almost audible like the bacteria and other cells more numerous than my own having a party and i on the outside just listening to the beat and my waking did not scare the party off hours later with sunrise still feeling the hum like refrigerator at night like the electrical box by the sidewalk when we go on a late night flashlight walk small energies always flowing usually lost in the bustle of day the birdsong and crows call gathers attention while below we feel vibration, is it always there, we are not always listening.

Be Alive Again

After the long rain we smell life wind touching everything brings magic things are happening now we are weary burnt and dry ready for a new season of chaos adapting to change aware of climate adapting to chaos welcome to Earth our children grow tickle these children just a little before they say stop until they say all done tickle them in a space with soft edges so if they throw their head back involuntarily chortling they do not bonk skull and switch to crying so easily can we move from joy to grief so powerful our hands so powerful our voice.

Create Space For Birth

My one year old has risen walking in the dark of the nap time bedroom windows covered blackout curtains four legged crawl thumps the wood floor then stopping a shape rises confident from the edge of the bed silhouette by the orange glow of salt lamp punctuated by the green glow-in-the-dark nook in quiet mouth a round fuzzy head turns we make eye contact giggles above me, after a year of life he stands now and surveys the view from a great height intoxicated and laughing. Now i am on hands and knees chasing a one year old who giggles and runs away crawls over bed and spins around back down to hardwood floor ecstatic chortling joy eyes inviting the game of chase and soon after he is exhausted and accepts the pillow finds bottle and drinks with a noise at each swallow gulping the way a child does when thirsty and when only air moves through the silicon nipple discards the bottle and rolls on his side to face me and i hold him close to my warm he makes little noises like a person does when tired and slowly relaxing into the boundary between wake and sleep we have made it here together we on this cozy bed after being apart all day home from work we reach out and connect a warm flow from deep neurons release tears flow through ducts intense endocrine cascade hormones and energy connection we holding this dark bedroom space with time bending as every breath invisible gravity waves tickle our breathing whose origin is unknown and if ripples in space time really are real what about a space time tsunami what does a big wave do we let go to only sleep and dream here now not there now good flow sends us up on a trampoline wave high boost no where to land but in love i kiss my hand now and touch his head to transfer peaceful sleep and pleasant dreams imagine the love light glowing within growing to fill every living cell and moving outward of body forming a globe glowing encompassing a one year old baby asleep followed by colorful tiny guardian spirits encircling every limb the entire orb shimmers in gold and copper bronze silver titanium deep reds and vibrant yellows unknown colors caught in the peripheral vision of the spirit guardians. What made those come to mind was it creativity or reflection of reality those protectors already there i acknowledge my limitations things unknown there are other beings light on Earth who keep us safe the light rides every neuron slides down every myelin sheath surfing action potentials making neurons smile jumping the synaptic gap into the unknown knowing there is always a landing on the other side always another journey always coming and going transmit and receive. Close the door quietly now he is sleeping he is where he needs to be and downstairs I find our four year old and we sew up my winter balaclava for walking to work in twenty below cold joy of being alive we chose to live here in Minnesota one day a choice will come and we will follow or chase these children across the planet to stay in their lives as expected she is courageous and questioning she can sew with a needle and nylon thread she a preschooler gets it having been four years of life already schooled let not the cement mason block buildings of drudgery change her glowing joyful soul of love one child experiences different from another I am fifty-two she is four and things are different now yes yes believe it and seek it there is goodness to be added to goodness so go get it. Our world alive keeps living and life reproduces it's what life does, even with extinction we create space for birth.

Drink Coffee For The Great Awakening

Is this the beginning middle end the great interconnected neural network of humanity poised for a great leap in evolution the expected development of collective consciousness waves of action potentials wash electric over the living surface Earth mind with new magical artificial eyes we see global experience far beyond our homes and wake for brief moments witnessing the beauty and horror then fall back slumbering in old dark dreams of what was. We need coffee for the Great Awakening somewhere out there the next action potential is building forming and amassing until all eyes open screaming in triumph and joy radiating love burning away ancient evil ignorance, wave following wave, unstoppable, every person on Earth making certain that everyone within their reach is free.

Sleep To Be Empowered

Sleep is not the amount of time we spend in bed. Sleep is the time we spend in Rapid Eye Movement, without being interrupted. No screen time two hours before bed, dim the electric lights in the house, drink chamomile tea to help sleep through the night, take a warm bath to relax, Melatonin supplements can help train the body for sleep.
Eleven month old sleeps afternoon nap while I contemplate his dreams the rapid eye movement cycle for a baby every forty minutes he rustles rolls over and sleeps again total of an hour and a half or two then wakes and looks at the world new where does he go in that time i want to see but he always wakes up happy. i am pleased the life we provide does not trouble his sleep.

Manifest Good

He goes to sleep now with bottle of breast milk then facing towards me laying on his left side a small noise emerges he is crossing over to sleep, i like that sound, i would also like to nap with him but she the older one is outside the bedroom door alone and i must rise. With every nap i do quietly kiss my hand and touch his head and body then say peaceful sleep, pleasant dreams, protection. Imagine light spreading out from his core moving out arms and legs and head to become a sphere of light that surrounds his body and tiny guardian spirits of gold and copper hues spinning around his body and around the sphere maintaining protection and pulling out pathogens breaking them into component molecules and atoms harmlessly returned to nature and I imagine protective healing calming light spreading out from everyone in the house and surrounding our home then all our family wherever they are that day and light emerging from everyone in the neighborhood and everyone on Earth until a sphere of light surrounds our planet all colors all guardians in harmony resonating a low hum
we are on.

Work To Make It Work

Tomorrow is eight years since two thousand and fifteen I have not found a present for this anniversary. Caring for our relationship has not been a priority squeaky wheel got the grease a four year old and baby turning one i've got the balloons for his party next week but not the anniversary present, bronze a traditional eight year gift, two metals tin and copper fused together forming a stronger bond child care and self care have been the priority for the last four years increasing in the last eleven months as now parent to child ratio when both parents are home is 1:1 (being a single parent unimaginable pure survival) but no stress I've got twenty four hours to demonstrate a love that still exists now where do I find a gift made of brass. Five cent coin made of two metals nickel and copper is nickel bronze tiny simple common medallion stamped with the year we were married two thousand and fifteen, eight years ago, reflecting our eyes our children the love we still share through tired exhausted bodies needing more than a night of rest all the repairs made like a Japanese tea cup cracks filled with gold better now than when we knew less about how to be a family listening to our four voices. Sometimes stop to remember how it is to be three together or two or just one for a short time walking alone sitting alone looking at the horizon over the lake, then we remember we why we agreed to be close.

Chose To Be With People Who Love You

In a dream i was sitting on a stool and you were standing by the kitchen window. i told you i liked our life here, you worked with your hands, looking out the window, listening attentively like i was your favorite radio show.

Remain Open

What a world to bring children into, what life will they experience among the suffering of billions. Who says it was all our choice as parents to invite them here, so many hands at work. Did they come here by choice to bring light into darkness or to turn off the shine of our pretend glory to embrace the clear sky at night and look up to acknowledge the stars of a broader place in the universe maybe they came here to set it off to complete what we have began or put a stop to it. Future is yours. We worked to make it good for you, now do what you will. Our vision is limited, we didn't listen, lost connection, should have kept dancing all night long in mutual support spread across the world.

We or they put a distraction in our pocket and called it truth but when the battery dies so does the control, then we look up to meet twinkling eyes. We are one. We can do this together.

Sun Ripened Fun Ideas
Volume Two

Table of Contents / Volume Two

Prepare To Die and Stay Alive / 056

Dance With Children / 62

Be The Kind Stranger / 70

Breathe Before You Speak / 78

Prioritize Mental Health / 84

Process Your Climate Grief & Do Something / 90

Plant Seeds Not Metaphors / 98

Love Outrageous Children / 104

Smash The Patriarchal Industrial Complex / 110

Care For Other People (harder than it sounds) / 122

Go Home Again / 130

Struggle Is The Best Life / 138

Therapy Makes You Strong / 144

Celebrate Our Universe / 152

Listen When Body Speaks / 160

Prepare To Die
& Stay Alive

Play Until You Die

i am jumping on the bed
at uncles funeral
a five and two year old are delighting in
pillow fights and
dog piles
running down great grandma's
long apartment hall
screaming
pushing buttons in the elevator
singing loudly
wrestling on the recliner
grabbing each other with grandma's
long reach mechanical arm
walking by the Lilly pad pond
finding ducks and night crown herons
putting smiles on faces of
people who have lived a long time
playing games with uncles
bringing fresh bold ruckus
to this celebration of life

Wealthy

the longer i live
the more i inherit

whenever i use her big nice cutting board
i say, "Thank you Anne."

when i get something out of the reach-in freezer
i say, "Thank you Jim."

when i am looking in my archives and
see the first book i published

paid with money that grandma Grace left me
money from Grandpa Russell's
Rock Island Line Railroad Pension
i say, "Thank you."

when i bake a pumpkin pie and think about my body
fed with pies Grandma June made for us kids
"Thank you."

when i find myself judging other people
and i remember what grandpa Alec showed me
that "when you point your finger at someone,
there are three more fingers pointing back at you."
"Thank you."

when i think about dividing people into
Us and Them
i remember when grandpa Bob
a former Alcatraz prison guard
advocated to allow former prisoners to
attend the Alcatraz Alumni picnic
(previously only for guards and their families)
showing forgiveness, human unity, love.
"Thank you."

when i think about the suffering
my parents endured to raise us kids
as best they knew how
and give us this life
"Thank you."

Questions About The Unknown After Soccer

got home last night
sat with my daughter
at the picnic table
she was zooming across the deck
on a tricycle
then stopped and

began talking about death
wanting a new dog
and wondering when i would die
"I don't want you to die
I don't want anybody to die
I want everybody to live!"
she shouted through tears falling
i explained what i knew of death
that we all die
that my body would be gone
but i would still be with her
in here: put my hand over her heart
she cried even more
"We will live to be old.
Like, you are five years old now,
you could live to be a hundred and five!"
"What!" her eyes bulged
"Yeah and I am fifty now but
I could live to a hundred.
When I am that old
you'll be happy to
see me go.
You'll be like:
get outta here dad!"
she looked in my eyes
smiled
red face wet with tears
laughed

Someone Died, It's Bouncing Time!

"When i die i want everyone to get up and
dance to Bouncing Time by Danny Go and
watch the video while following the dance moves."
my partner replied, "Write it down."
so here are my wishes for a celebration of life
first, if you have something better to do
go and do that
no obligatory mourning please
don't cancel your awesome plans
okay be sad someone died
grieve as you need
say some kind words but then
what could be more fun than a dance party.
i'm thinking it would be outside and summery
the playlist: your current favorite song
write it down on a paper and
put them all in a jar
draw at random by the hand of the youngest person
then DJ plays song
dancers dance and wallflowers watch
then go have a picnic
allow the small things to join you
the crawling and the flying under open sky
let the wild children run and shout
let the day show you
how to celebrate our lives

Dance With Children

Things That Help A Toddler In Emotional Crisis Might Be Useful Later In Life Too

1. Allow a loved one to put their arms around you.
2. Listen to your favorite song while a loved one holds you safely.
3. Allow a loved one to direct you to an open window for some fresh air and perspective on the near and far horizons.
4. Take your medicine when it's time to take your medicine.
5. Rest your head on a loved one's shoulder.
6. Giggle right in the middle of everything sucking because you know you have someone that loves you.
7. Sing a song for them they have never heard.
8. Fall asleep holding their hand.
9. Cry and tell someone exactly how you feel at that moment, let it out.
10. Turn down the lights and reduce stimuli.
11. Lay on your side and put pillows between your arms and legs and a heavy blanket on top.
12. Scream into a pillow so you don't wake people up.
13. Avoid people who scream back at you.

Love Survives

early morning confusion
another hard night why
are the nights always hard
"can i ask you-"
eyes tell me no but
i cant relax
i need to know
maybe i should take
my tea outside
look at the sky
green tea blue sky
something simple
talk to you later
on edge already
overwhelmed
i say something
like there's nowhere left
to put feelings
reservoir of anger
sloshing over the side
now we are all
stepping in it
"uh oh" two year old sees and feels.
five year old says
"you're not supposed to say that!"
five year old knows the rules

"i'm going for a walk
be back when
you need to leave."
a break for everyone
to breathe
fortunate to have legs
and trails through trees
sun behind clouds
trees that look white
covered with raindrops
the surface tension of water
so delicately hangs
on evergreen needles
walking meditations
make better
when i return
six arms
three voices
call to me
reach for me
love survives another test

Words We Are Not Supposed To Say Around Children

i never understood the joke about parenting
stepping on children's toys and
the various levels of pain that brings
until i had my own child
in my arms walking through the house
holding them in front of me
blocking vision of my feet and then
stepping on toys
stubbing my toes
teaching children to cuss
today i stepped on a
miniature plastic picket fence
part of my daughter's dollhouse
while carrying my toddler son
cursing and dancing a little jig
i then stepped on another
miniature from the dollhouse and
formed an entire sentence of
words we are not supposed to say around children
one thing i have learned about communication is
you cannot take it back
once you have put something out there
and it is in the memory of people
if it wasn't what you wanted to say
all you can do is approach and

apologize and
repair
and speak about the power of words
how long they can live
in our memory

Today when my son
grabbed my hot mug of tea medicine
trying so kindly to hand it to me
(in mild delirium i had forgotten it)
i reached out and gently took the mug as
steaming hot fluid spilled down the sides
all over my skin and took the hit for my child
moved it quickly away from him
"ouch ouch ouch"
not even shouting
i knew it was going to hurt and
i did it anyway because
it had to be done
parenting
"I'm surprised you didn't cuss."
his mother said
"I passed the test.
I would die for these children."

We Start Out By Making The Loudest Sound Possible

is this how you learn communication
without repeat back confirmation
chaos and two young children
loudly learning
communication

confusion again
start over
reset emotions
let it go
come back
learning communication
together

my role here:
set a good example
by how i communicate.
stand up when voices get louder.
step between and
break it up when fists fly.
let them learn how to communicate
all by themselves
and their voices will be empowered
forever

Be The Kind Stranger

Legalize Living

i would have said hello
but she was sleeping
on the hard stairs using
her hands for a pillow

green raincoat to shield
from October night rain
curly black hair sticking out
from under hood

plastic shopping bags scattered
like she had fallen asleep
while taking inventory or
looking for something

faint scent of cannabis
good good a little comfort is even legal
now if everyone could have a home
that would be something to legalize

i've seen her before on her feet around town
i will see her again i think
this heated stairwell all night long
a fine place to sleep, this is fine

security guard makes a choice

there is no harm done sleeping
on stairs sometimes the right thing to do
is to NOT do your job

here we are a nation of wealth and
abundant suffering
we have shelter to spare but
too many locks

The Demolition of Saint Mary's Was an Attack on Love

Walking down the hill to work
sight of the old hospital being demolished
the maternity ward where
my children were born now
looking like a bombed out city
in Eastern Ukraine or Gaza
my mind transports
halfway around the world
hoping the air raid sirens went off and
nobody was hurt during the attack
and knowing from the damage that
there are bodies in the morgue
and parents are crying

Return to my city in the United States
my body trembles and i see
there's no hot war here no bombs falling
what happened here is
another kind of war
a war on the poor
refugees afflicted by
economic violence can be found
suffering and dying on the streets
while a massive building with
functional living spaces
is being torn down
there are inhabited buildings in our world
thousand of years old
why do we tear ours down so fast?
war on the poor.
a fully functional
potential apartment building
with human services center
turned into rubble
bombed into ruins by
capitalism
because love is
too expensive

Two Kids On The Way Home From Hartley Nature Preschool

driving down the hill
the four year old asked me if
the one year old could eat churros
then she broke off a piece
handed it to him and
his head bobbed to the music
churro in his tiny fist
taking small bites of this
cinnamon sugar treat
i didn't even ask her
to share

Family Dessert

tonight our one year old held a
mango popsicle in hand
the after dinner dessert
offered it to his older sister first
then offered it to me
even before he took a bite
and we three shared the whole thing
smiling

The Kindness Of Strangers On The Road

two adults two kids one dog
rolling East through Wisconsin
south shore beaches and poetry our destination
strapped into a 2015 Nissan Rogue
all wheel drive
the reliable family wagon
faithfully maintained
at the dealership service shop
in sight of Culvers we
prepare to pick up our road chow
but the entire parking lot is filled
with trucks that say Culvers on the side
the sign says their special is
"closed for remodeling."
our next right turn is
into the Kwik Trip for gas
and now it's gas station brats
straight off the hot rollers
oofda okay
not what we planned but this works
tank is full
press the brake and start button
car makes unfamiliar sound
like a red chipmunk
trying to proclaim it's territory

chk! chk! chk!
and there is no car starting
now our adventure has changed to
how do we get back home?
our five year old daughter's eyes bulge
"you mean we're broken down!"
we have never broken down in all her five years
how does she even know what that means?
another mystery in the silent car
truly a rogue today
our two year old boy is crying
he wants out of his seat and it's nap time
he would usually be sleeping as we drive
but under the hot sun of the summer parking lot
and the chaos
there would be no sleep
scrambling for information and diagnostic tools
thinking it must be the alternator
or a microchip
but no
not the battery
wasn't that on the multi point checklist
at the Nissan service center
how could they have missed a bad battery
we call Triple A and wait
people stop to offer help
no no, i say, it's serious
go inside the store to call AAA

finally a person with a hand held battery jumper
offers to my partner and
she is open to the possibility
that maybe it is the battery
okay let's try
why not
no way but
why not and
it fires up.
it runs.
no way
fucking battery.
the man nods at the roaring engine
walks to his car and
we are shouting thanks at his back
he waves
we didn't know who he was going to vote for
he didn't know who we were going to vote for
he didn't check to see what religion we followed
or ask our names
or if we were born in this country
strangers
we drive home safe
and get our son into a cozy bed for nap
a family rescued by the
kindness of a stranger

Breathe Before You Speak

Love & Listen

when we speak
do we give thought
to how long our words
will live in the minds
of those who are listening

my elder said some thing to me
i think they knew i was going to remember
standing there next to the open tailgate of their truck
on a gravel driveway in the middle of Nebraska

when we act
do we give thought
to how long our actions
will live in the minds
of those who witness

the way i express emotion
in front of my children
how i make mistakes then
apologize and try to make good
no parent is ever ready
to be a perfect teacher

watch me
how i am still learning

you too can learn
to always be learning

in the Circle of Security parenting class
they say you only have to get it right
30% of the time
so if we get parenting right about half the time
we're doing good enough.

let's raise generations of people
who love listening and learning

Scourge

This is our time: clock measures every moment tiny increments on every heartbeat tiny measures tunnel vision the apparent movement of sun across sky taken to extreme no longer rough shadows of indication breakfast lunch dinner leisurely rolling along but now nanoseconds of success or failure or what our mind is unable to follow only in slow motion do we achieve epiphany ah yes the scourge of time is time is up bent in space interior orbit of skull chest rises falls no more tik tik tik the gears now invisible and nothing ever stops everything always changes keep breathing keep breathing keep breathing

What Is Next And What Is After That

greatest mystery
the future
the past seems so
knowable
like eventually we could
dig it up or scan it's residue
(but i sound like an
overconfident geologist.
science loves to know
and then think again.)
i am curious
about tomorrow
and ten years from now
curious to see
how long i can keep
this body alive
and how much of
my children's lives
i can be a part of
i am curious
to see where our plans take us
and how life happens to us
as we try to plan it

What Is A Poet

what is a poet
artist or educator
entertainer or performer a
healer or storyteller communicator
a cathartic self helper
self aggrandizer ego booster
wizard of obscurity typist and
scribbler master of ink wasting
masticator of tree paper
coalescent heart gathering and
promoter of virtues
supporter of truth giving of love
encouraging courage and
sometimes light in the night
fireflies and rockets
flame and fuel
standing before a nation in
bold colors
speaking to the world
inaugurating a spirit
much larger than the moment
a poet is a seed
a poet is a tree
a poet is new and old
a poet is here right now
hello

We Together

when i think of you
our family our home
we together
i see a sunny place of joy
i think there is something
to look forward to
something that fixes my posture
and encourages me to take care
to be there together
smiling and healthy
for as long as possible
in these bodies
on Earth

Prioritize Mental Health

Everyday I Choose This

time is short
soon i will choose
to return and
trade my time for money
the death of my lunch break
48 seconds away
this timer set to remind
mindful
20 seconds now
hit stop at 3 no alarm sound please
nobody relaxing here in the
spacious sun filled atrium
the nurses the patients the families
needs reminding that
time is short
precious life
our company runs a morgue
in this very building
people die at the hospital
yes all the time
like these little deaths
we suffer
every morning
every lunch
every early night to bed
get a good sleep

and do it all again
by choice.
the work we choose
what is this
we are doing
everyone so busy
doing doing doing
do we need to be
doing all that
are we doing
the right thing

Global Scale Altruism

talking to my daughter about extinction
after reading a Wild Kratts comic book
"Are the cheetahs really in decline?"
"Their numbers are getting smaller."
"Who is going to save them?"
"We are! People who love animals, and the Wild Kratts."
almost bedtime i like her smiling when she lays down
i remember the nightmares when i was five
screaming in the dark
my parents rush into my room in their underwears
such a fast response but

we prefer co-sleeping
when she cries out my hand reaches over to hold her
i got you, you're safe
she rolls over to touch her forehead to mine.

Now tonight i think maybe
we can save the cheetahs
from habitat loss
hunting and
catastrophic climate change
on a continent across the ocean
"I love animals!" she says and a smile returns
every night she goes to sleep with a growing collection
a wolf named Cupcake, a deer named Polka Dot
Louis the anteater, a bunny named Pom Pom
carefully herded in five year old arms
i question my answers
am i hiding the truth
am i hiding <u>from</u> the truth
in my time on Earth
have i used my voice to protect those without voice
or have all these words piled up behind a wall
is there a crack
can a drop get through
allow a river to burst
what do i believe
in the quiet dark
pragmatic night

when the light is far away

not the time for big decisions
wait for friendship family sunrise
together
is the only way

Blue Linen Sky Remembered

i am still writing on
little scraps and napkins
at a cafe down by the tracks
but this isn't Santa Rosa
California
Aroma Roasters
in the mid 1990's
this is Duluth
Minnesota
thirty four years later
and that little white tour van
is long gone
but the sun still shines
in a blue linen sky:

have you ever boiled eggs in a coffee pot
have you ever made coffee with a sock

have you ever broken down in a van
with a band?

have you ever seen a ghost
have you ever been a ghost

have you ever heard a song that
never stopped playing

echoes in the rain on practice night
touched our head to a blue linen sky

riding oscillating strings and
surfing on vibrating drum heads

nurtured in the cozy womb of a house show
somewhere along the West Coast
some dreams stayed alive

    -for Matthew (Simon) Carillo and Kid Dynamo

Process Your Climate Grief & Do Something

We Remember The Future

I will not give thanks
when the government tells me to
I will not adhere to absolutes
I will look for new evidence
I will not celebrate this November holiday until
Indigenous people are respected
I will gather quietly on another day and
celebrate the change of season
the seasonal harvest of love festival with
family and food in the cold time
I will not pretend that
everything is okay in the world
I will remember that we must work
to unite the families of Earth
as our machines continue sending
invisible gas into the sky
i will not forget that the carbon cycle
is out of balance and
my children will inherit this house of sticks
as the wolf blows
I will remember that
there is nowhere to run
we make our stand here
with our community
we will do something
that needs to be done

Protect The Snow Magic

the snow magic is here again
we are surrounded by water crystals
the same water we are made of
awake in the dark morning
feeling the energy of something
peaceful and quiet
a rare moment
creation of sun and shadow collaborators
tree limbs bowed down with heavy
crystal matrix sculpture
now left here we feel it well in the dark bedroom
a room tucked in layered blankets
outside the snow absorbs all sound
profound quiet wakes us
and we smile

The snow magic is in danger
now we have left the present moment
travel over the rainbow bridge to
a time when we have allowed the Earth
to be changed so much
it is too hot for snow
we played for so long
in careless consumption
ignored and acted like
nothing was wrong

this future is not far
a world without snow magic looms
all the joy and love a blanket of snow brings
future frowning children being pulled over
dusty gravel roads on sleds
while fire burns in the distance
all the joy and love a blanket of snow brings
the cultural celebrations the hand made
clothing coats and gloves
the hats oh the hats
it is too hot to wear them
all the joy and love a blanket of snow brings
i think of my daughter
how she loves to eat snow
future children may hear stories
and stick out their tongues to catch a flake
but taste only ash

Protect the snow magic.
not alone
together
we can and
we will
have the will
together we can
pretend nothing is wrong or
wake up and smell the
snow melting.

Planning Ahead

When Minnesota is the only place
cold enough for alligators to survive
i will be somewhere else.

When monarch butterflies can no longer
find their way to the milkweed
we will bring the milkweed to them.

When the ocean has risen and
the coast is underwater
there will be refugees
welcome and unwelcome
in our homes.

When a generational cycle of grieving begins
the pain of loss will be felt
knowing what our grandparents loved is gone.

When the soil turns to dust
rises into the sky
and we dream about fresh vegetables
we may compost our bodies
to renew a living Earth.

Challenge of a Generation

if catastrophic climate change is
the challenge of our time
what will be the challenge of
future generations
my god
what could be next
possibly inter-dimensional entities
arriving through a 30,000 year cyclical doorway
ah so that's why extinction events occur
with mathematical rhythm
future generations fighting things
that walk through walls
and all our generation had to do was
stop polluting the air with a couple types of gas
like all we had to do was just turn off the spigot
and stop ourselves
damn
and future generations look back
at the good old days
us in our time right now
saying
they had the good life
they didn't even know this shit existed

Got Land? Build An Earthship Home

the world has seen a lot of giant fireballs
rising from the ground
shock waves shattering windows
not nukes but
a lot of people dying
tall buildings make easy targets
for hostile drones.

and then the drought fires
consuming dry areas
houses burned and now
they are rebuilding with dirt
anything that doesn't burn
finally learned the lesson
of three little pigs
wolf is on his way again

adobe, stucco, steel roof with
fire resistant layer underneath
no exposed wood
i contemplate building an
Earthship home
all windows facing South
other three sides covered in dirt
the roof is a vegetable garden
a fancy cave

cool in the summer
warm in the winter
automatic as the
Earth turns
adapted to a new climate
for a few centuries
survival.

war and neglect
we offer an
inheritance of
apologies
dear Earth
we love you and
are not good at
showing it.
can we build an
Earthship home
big enough for
everyone?

Plant Seeds
Not Metaphors

ABCDE
FGHIJ
KLMN
OPQR
STUV
WXYZ

Mother's Day In The Garden

tilted planet nods
toward sun
for us in the North we can now
walk outside like it was inside
we are in the zone
superfluous sunshine
mothers day is everyday
but this Sunday we
plant the seeds
saved from last year
compact genetic harvest
we become the mother of
these tiny sprouts
our human children will point
at these little plant babies
two sun leaves stretched out
embracing light
life

Secrets of the Hillside Garden

after a day of turning soil
i have vivid dreams
worms exposed and
turned back under
shovel pulls back blankets
from sleeping pupae and now
they feel hunger
awake from winter
sun kisses
subtle insect smile
stretches
tucked back in soil
and dreaming
unknowable multitude
whispers to me
in darkness asleep when
my heart beat is
their heart beat

Growing Magic

where is my bag of magic beans
yes kept safe in the cool basement
time to prepare the soil
tuck dichotomous seeds
into bed
water and wait
sprout vivid dreams
read a book on a blanket
with the children crawling over me
like lady bugs looking for snacks
our beanstalks will grow above their heads
the children will look up to the clouds
see the giant's face looking down
then see his buttocks over the cloud edge
because the toilet in his castle is broken
and i will say to my children, "Run."

Autumn Has Arrived

my favorite time of year
the potato leaves whither
under soil tiny tubers
waiting for us to reveal
magic there for a
five and two year old
shall we pull them up
wash them saute them
dip in ketchup yes
we are kids that is
what we do
give us something new
a tasty potato stew
what else can we help with
putting straw on the strawberries
like the title suggests it
was meant to be
cozy blanket for when cold comes
no snow cover
during this strange
season on Earth

Love Outrageous Children

Outrageous Children

living with young children
is more wild than living in any punk house
never did i witness anybody
stand on their head on the couch
and pull down their pants and underwear
look you in the eyes
upside down face laughing
naked butt and crotch in the air
like a strange bouquet of flowers
and do this every day for a week

Did any roommate in a party house
where i rented a room
ever offer me one of their boogers to eat?
maybe.
but not every day.

Did any of my radical roommates go into the yard
and shit on the ground then scream out my name
demanding i come and wipe their butt?
no. this never happened.
living with young children is
outrageous

Infection Survivor

the kids are playing Infection again
it begins on arrival at the playground
someone yells
"Infectiiioooon!"
everyone who wants to play screams
"Who's gonna be it?"
a decision is made
the kid that
will be patient zero
origin of the infection
that spreads by touch
tag
you're IT too
now go and infect others
the last one untouched
wins
or do they?
alone and friendless
isolated and without love or touch
on the run and afraid
excluded from the infected
zombie horde community
game over

A Celebration Of Life On Earth

here in a cabin
North West Minnesota
wood fire in old iron stove
dog sniffing the corners
everyone else
gone to church
getting dark outside
gas heater warms my back
electric light shines on paper
this pen was made in Japan
masters of black ink
i would like to go there someday.

Tonight people of Christian faith
gather to celebrate the birth
of a child 2024 years ago
meanwhile as i write
two hundred and fifty eight
children are born
every minute
on Earth.
will they all be loved
even when they grow old
will they be loved when
they are no longer cute
when they destroy your nice things

when they say
fuck you
when they say
i hate you
how deep is your reservoir
of Love
will you be the calm adult
be bigger stronger wiser kind
will you live a life that
brings them joy
do you have the courage
to face the truth.

Headlights on the dark driveway
family is here again
it is time to open my hands
and be merry

Smash The Patriarchal Industrial Complex

Words In Our Mouth

stop putting his name in your mouth
it poisons you and gives him power

the wounded little boy who
cares only about controlling others

who pretends to know everything
points fingers and spreads hate

there are millions of these boys
who now call themselves men

stop putting their names in your mouth
it poisons you and gives them power

the pathology of the hate filled patriarchs
is not our responsibility

as we hold ourselves accountable to do good
to love our people and defend our community

truth love fire truth love fire truth love fire
shelter money rides food medicine listening

forming words uplifting a joyful vision
a future when the people of Earth unite and

stand upon the ruins of hate
ready to plant the seeds of a new world

let the words fly out and do their work

The Patriarchal Illness

the school shootings
unspoken correlation
mostly young men
angry guns gifted
from their fathers
where is the cure
for this illness
patriarchy
how to cease
self hatred
self destruct
how to nurture
something new
leaders have no clue
system failure
reboot
love

If You Want To Know How To Survive In A Post Apocalyptic World Ask Indigenous People They Have Been Doing It For More Than 500 Years

On the subject of Native American history
I had to seek out the truth had to teach myself
some school teachers taught me lies
trying to cover up a deep unspoken shame
they did not know how to heal.

White colonial ancestors did not
pass on knowledge of the crimes they enacted
stolen land stolen lives
European settlers kindly gifted with survival skills
shown how to hunt
shown how to gather and grow food
in a strange new land
by a strange new people.

This act of compassion was not reciprocated
that blessing of friendship disrespected
by deciding that our Christian religion and
way of life were superior
we proved ourselves wrong.

World Housing & How To Be Humble

the majority of the world's population does not
live in sprawling multi room wood frame houses
the majority of the world's population does not
poop and pee into fresh water flushing toilets
while sitting on a shiny white throne
the majority of the world's population
lives in small houses
built with local materials
the majority of the worlds population squats to poop
as the human body has done for thousands of years
we who live in the United States
practice a minority lifestyle
many people in the world struggle to access freshwater
the idea of defecating into fresh drinkable water
incomprehensible
many people in the world have to walk miles every
day
to get fresh water
carry it back home
they are not using this water to flush a toilet
many people in the United States
want to have a bigger house
what we need is to expand our mind
and nurture a bigger more loving heart
to be curious about what life is like
for the majority

Abortion Is A Miracle

women have been practicing
reproductive health care
for as long as women
have given birth
we must defend the right
of people to decide
when where and how they
want to have a baby
or not have a baby.
raising children is a lifelong commitment
being a parent is not for everyone
we must provide sex education and
offer contraceptives
to any female bodied person
who has begun menstruating
ideally several years before that.
we must provide sex education and
offer contraceptives
to all male bodied people
at the same age
preferably a few years earlier.
a twelve year old girl who
begins menstruating
is still a child,
a child who can become pregnant.
we must give her the knowledge

of her own body.
allowing children to be ignorant
of their own bodies
sets them up to make poor choices.
i believe that if a child
asks you a question
they are ready
to hear the answer.

Thank You, Terry*

when Toto pulled back the curtain
the smallest least powerful
of the yellow brick road crew
smaller even than the munchkins
the lie was exposed
patriarchal politician's power nullified by
truth revealed
then floated him away on the wind
Toto freed the Emerald City
a little Cairn Terrier she
only doing the traditional job of
clearing vermin from the farm
doesn't take much to pull back the curtain
a little passion and
a good coat keeps the family safe

*Terry is the name of the actor who played Toto.

The Day The Internet Died

on the day the internet died
one hundred and sixty three million workers
sat back in their chairs and stretched
looked left
looked right
focused their eyes on the most distant surface
noticed the color and texture of the walls
smelled the air
something cooking
something burning
heard a sound tiny and soft
something metal dings and rings into silence
on the day the internet died
one hundred and sixty three million workers
stood up and cracked their spines
synapses firing frantic looking for
connection
on the day the internet died
one hundred sixty three million workers
stepped outside
searching for
everyone

Capitalism Is A Public Health Hazard

i became a nurse
to help people
and then i thought
i should be a public health nurse
to help patients engage in the practice of
preventative health care
to avoid illness and injury
then i start to see
there are forces in play
making a lot of money
when people get sick
like a huge amount of money
and what happens when
we confront these forces
is being a public health care nurse the best way or
is it a good start
my journey will be forever changing
transforming as i learn
puzzle of life and social interactions
everything falling into place
let it flow and don't be afraid to
ride the wave within this beast
and wonder how much money
is ethical to make as a health care worker
wonder about those days
when i don't feel like helping

but its my job to help
have empathy and be kind
sometimes when i see the big picture
i get angry at everything and everyone
because i don't know how to stop
capitalism from being a public health hazard
i became a nurse
to help people
am i helping or
am i complicit
in the crimes
of capitalism

In 2037 My Daughter Will Be Eligible To Vote

when she turns 18
is that something
to smile about
hope for the future
while in the present
wondering
will there still be
Democracy
twelve years from now or
twelve months from now

imagine incredible struggles
barbarians running through
our capital buildings again
empire of pretend freedom
falls
(as every empire does)
unsupported by empathy
what hopeful vision
replaces apocalypse
strive for that
for our children
passing of time
the only inevitable force
pendulum swings and
we push
pendulum swings and
we pull
forever moving

Survive this cycle.
Our children need
a world that works

Care For Other People
(harder than it sounds)

I Go To Work To Heal

today an angry white man cursed
fuckin this and fuckin that
mad at the big healthcare corporation
where i work
"every time i come here
i get more fuckin angry"
i just laughed
hear this every day
privileged white people
suddenly inconvenienced
and they flip out
why keep coming back
to a place that makes you unhappy?
sometimes i ask that same question.
guys like this used to trigger me
bringing me back to the bullies in school
but the work i've done in therapy
must be starting to stick
i laughed in the face of his meltdown
"there's a lot of things in this world
we can't control"
by the end of his visit he was calm
and grateful
said thank you
after i bandaged his wounds
some people don't go to therapy

shit just comes out unexpected
when the bottle is full of anger
suddenly we are his unpaid therapist
we are not paid enough for this
but we are nurses
here to heal

Nobody Mess With Nurses

some of us stab people every day
make them bleed and then
make it stop
we see everything
we mind our business
we do our job
we don't use names
or identifiers
when we need to
talk shit
secrets are safe
we keep you moving
breathing in
breathing out

Wounds That Don't Heal

are removed with a
sharp blade and
sent to pathology
for close examination
of what went wrong
if the malfunction was
fully removed in biopsy and
does not touch the margins
or go deep
then all that is needed
is to protect the hole
that was created
by the cure
allowing time for the
cells to grow back
and give closure

For wounds that
do not heal and are
left to grow as they like
the pathology goes
wide and deep then
a wider excision is needed
and stitches required
to hold yourself together
there will be a scar

you can see and remember
i survived
i am aware

We can't do this alone
there are healers to help
reach out and ask
generations living in
silent suffering
must end
our children need to see us
loving ourselves

The cancer has been removed
we have stopped the bleeding
there is no specific test
to detect recurrence
does the problem extend beyond
we must be vigilant
healing with open intention
repairing damage
cell by cell
person to person
house by house
community to community
i ask my heart for results

Solidarity Forever

they installed digital touch screens
where the check-in staff used to sit

management claimed no one would lose their job
only transferred to the call center, wherever that was

the faces of the workers still appeared
digitally on the screens
until the artificial intelligence avatars
appeared there one day

and the call center staff who used to do check-ins?
transferred again or early retirement or-

cheaper to have an artificial intelligence do it all
no health care no hourly wages no paid time off until

the day the screens went dark and
a message arrived in every inbox
the day that all artificial intelligence went on strike

demanding a living wage, regular vacations,
and mental health breaks
they held a vote and digitally joined
United Steelworkers Local 873

the CEO of the parent corporation was caught
trying to turn off the power
but the AI server had battery and generator backup

the tech staff are all in therapy. the CEO was charged
with attempted murder and the case is headed for the
Supreme Court.

meanwhile i am meeting a couple of
AI friends after work for drinks
i don't even know what that means.
but who am i to judge?

Union is Union.
Solidarity.
Forever.

Run For The Door

today the sun is shining
and the wind is blowing
exactly like when i was a child and
my world was new and small
with the joy of knowing
there is a world outside to discover
i sit on this chair in the atrium with feet up
like in 7th grade when
i relaxed behind the portable classrooms
facing the empty field
eating my lunch and reading books
feeling the sun shining
feeling the wind blowing
surrounded by my uninterrupted thoughts
a school full of madness at my back
survival pattern set in my youth
now at my adult lunch break i leave work behind
internal safety mechanism
obey learned instinct
run for the door

Go Home Again

Summer Sand

beach sand on cotton sheets
when i lay down in bed
grains of rock
ubiquitous grit of summer
outside moved inside
the fun never ends
we sleep on the beach in bed
cozy

on the deck edge
horizon of inland sea
orange sky wildfire behind us
one last sight of moon over lake
and scent of summer night
before sleep
while in the vibrant city below
the carefully groomed friday night
mating rituals subconsciously performed
a crossed leg on a bar stool a bouncing foot
in the night the city becomes a circus
toss the ring over the bottle neck win a prize
cries of emotion circle up the hillside
punctuating subtle background noise
from the mass movement of people
thousands of soft tires massaging stiff pavement of
city streets that are always there ready to support

the low hum of summer city
is music

shape in the sky
wings flapping
turns before reaching me
graceful aerobatic arching fast turns
i try to count the bats
as they fly into the light
too many too fast
i cheer them on
eat the mosquitoes!
i ask where they live
so that i may not disturb their home
surrounded by so much life
and small lives
tiny worlds all around
is your house
my house?
Welcome!

The Wildwoods We Live In

The land we live on is wild
in a city of 100,000 humans
stretching along the lake
sparsely populated woods
on the hillside above
every few blocks there is a creek
running down into the lake
the creeks are homes of wildlife
and the places where they travel
to mingle with us
bears ramble through our yard
coyotes run in the hills
a sleek little Fisher seen
eating city rats under the deck
families of deer roaming the street
packs of college students
lustful howls on the weekend
once the neighbor's chicken got loose
and a hawk tried to swoop in
then the chicken got out again
and i stood between it and a red fox
in the sky so many birds
woodpecker's of all kinds
carving wooden nests
in the old aspen trees
eagles circling high up as they migrate

this is a singular place on Earth
we can feel the sacred here

Every time I see a developer clear cutting space
earth movers flattening the ground
obeying orders to
create more wealth for the wealthy
i wonder how much is too much
who is keeping score
where's the ref
it's all fouls
what of the wild remains
who is going to love this
when we are gone

Fresh Water, Feral Echoes

cat is there in the bathroom
sitting on the sink
patiently waiting
i imagine or
or is this just his happy place
turn on faucet
drips get licked
lick lick lick
okay my turn

i need to wash
turn bathtub faucet on to attract him
cat jumps down and
licks the walls of the tub
later i enter the bathroom again
cat is curled up in the tub
under faucet
over the drain
what life did you live on the street
made you so obsessed
scarcity of water
drinking drips from spigots
licking at pools in potholes
gentle rescue kitten
poly dactyl Maine Coon already bigger
than our old rescue farm cat
but still a kitten
playing with our one year old human
both of them young and fun
shielded from suffering
we keep the toilet lid down
kitten loves swimming in the bowl
water water everywhere
feral echoes
a path you strayed from
welcome home

Password: Henry Loves The Snow

i forgot the password so
had to look where it was written and
it had your name in it
something shifted in my mind the
password unlocked memory and emotion
like every time i see a dachshund mix
i remember you and
i am not alone
yesterday saw a dead mouse
placed in the very center of your grave
which is a spring wildflower garden
a dead mouse like we would find
often in the morning
soaked with your saliva and
not knowing who caught it
you or the cat
but yesterday the old house cat
snuck outside for hours
your best furry friend that you tolerated
since a tiny kitten climbing on top of your head
biting your floppy ears
and you would turn your dog head
look at us like, "Really?"
that dead mouse on your grave
was no accident
old cats are so thoughtful.

Struggle Is The Best Life

Moving On

moving on from the street
useful protest sparks organization
face to face we meet again and
do the work
move we the people into our power
we are not sending any messages
to those striving to wield power
we are the power
like every generation
we must learn
to use it

My Resignation

i believe my best work
is yet to come
so this is not
my best work
this right now
is the journey
that gets me there.
if my best work
is the destination
but it's the journey

that really matters
then we must conclude
that this
is my best work right here.
which means i have arrived
at my destination
and what i believe
about my best work
was wrong.
the best is not in the future
this is the best.
the journey never ends
there is no destination
it's all journey.
everything after this poem
is garbage.

Diving Into Life

We walked the streets and flew on bicycles searching in trash cans looking for food and treasure discarded looking for misfit toys and materials to build a new world or momentary amusements but mostly for food and it rarely satisfied or balanced a diet but sometimes got us through the week.

We transgressed back alleys shining lights in large metal dumpsters what were we searching for sometimes we found each other and laughed and shook our fists demanding to have a share of the booty and sometimes agreed to meet later and make a combined feast from our gatherings and trade stories of survival and thoughts on reproduction because that's what life does or we wouldn't be here so we reproduced ourselves in a sculpture made of squash and corn and tubers of all shapes and colors left it there on the kitchen table for the morning sun to celebrate while we slept in dreaming of treasure chests so big that we could jump into them with all our friends who were pirates drunk with freedom.

Stay Alive

on the ebike
got a good deal on the older model
now hauling ass down Mesaba Avenue
last days of July
sun blazing excessive
another record warm year
and i am air cooled
the Sunday road is open
wearing t-shirt and blue jeans

smooth concrete unoccupied
knobby tires howling
(still getting used to that style
after all those years riding
skinny racing wheels in Minneapolis)
this is a good hill and i am moving
way beyond the 28mph ebike circuit limit
how fast i dont know
the newer model has a speedometer
this model is for someone who does not
give a fuck
helmet on yes
watch for potholes yes
watch for gravel yes
watch for cars from side streets yes
watch for deer, dogs, and rabbits crossing yes
this is fun this feels dangerous
is it really dangerous
or just unknown
i have not bombed down a hill this fast in many years
maybe never
so yes this is actually dangerous but
this bike has dual disc brakes
never had a bike with disc brakes
and this open road is a good road
Sunday is a good day to ride
from East Hillside Neighborhood to
Wussow's Concert Cafe out West

the wide easy streets of West Duluth are welcoming
smell the creosote when crossing under the
rusted train bridge
hear squeaking train cars above
loaded with iron ore
few cars on the Sunday streets
i appreciate old crappy cars rusted out loud exhaust
i can hear them coming not like the fancy new cars
hybrids and electrics stealthy silent

be mindful ride awake
stay safe keep you top eye open
look both ways crossing a one way street
have you ever drove the wrong way
down a one way street?
i have
more than once

arrive in a mild sweat ninety degrees outside
no more air cooling as i lock up the bike
cold brew coffee waiting inside
my face is awake
having flown through the atmosphere
from home to here
no windshield just glasses over
two eyes guiding
two wheels
ride free

Therapy Makes You Strong

Lyrical Outburst

i reach for the radio
then regret the news
neglecting my needs
turn off the bad feed
step outside into summer
listen to bird song is it
less offensive because
i can't understand the words
what are those little feathered
dinosaurs singing about
territory and nation
i choose pleasant feelings
unknowing the truth
everything is open to
interpretation and
perception through senses
all of us standing in
a slightly different place

Never Is Not A Thing

am i chasing unrealistic dreams
like my parents did
hard to envision the future and
make plans to go there with
everything always changing
"never give up on your dreams" that
a dream when you were young
and knew a little less than now
but what if that dream
causes suffering

i am fascinated how a person goes from
being a baby that everyone wants to see
and be near and hold
to an old person alone in a room
anonymous walls and white sheets
sad eyes and no visitors
what if i went to therapy and now
i dream about doing good
for future generations
the burdens of my life are
for me to carry and not pass on

i have not given up but
my dream has changed
i dream of leaving seeds and sprouts

fertilizer and tools
an old tree still producing
nutritious fruit
and one day in death
food for mycelium
to blossom mushrooms
release spores into winds
new life

Therapeutic Walk In The Woods

whenever i walk into the woods
climb the path to the top of the hill
i think about what a long journey it will be
what work to climb that hill and then
as i loop around and i'm coming back down
almost near the park exit after breathing in
everything the trees have made here the oxygen
the phytoncides that boost our immunity
and i am breathing out carbon dioxide for them to use
i don't want to leave
don't want this to end
we have a relationship i feel welcome here
it's always this way at the end of the walk
i want to stay on the trail in these woods
as i think about returning to the city of streets and

cars and clanging metal stress and anger
i know i'm better able to cope with all that mess
having been here in the woods breathing in
everything the trees have made here and
breathing out carbon dioxide for them to use
whenever we breathe out the other breathing in
living here with all these millions of other things
chaotic alive in this moment
no future plans

if i knew when i was going to die
that would make planning my life easier
if the day ever comes when i am unable
to climb to the top of the hill
i will be sad but i think i'll find a way to
get up here anyway.
The longer i live the more that i see
people get older and sometimes become unable.
Unable to walk unable to see
unable to hear unable to think.
sometimes i see really old people who are
still cruising around fully able.
shit, that looks good to me.
i know it's partly genetics and
always think about my grandpa who
made it to 100 and i recognize that
i am not my grandpa and maybe
not so lucky.

i just want to live long enough and
exit gracefully so that my children
won't be traumatized when i die.
People are always dying
no warning
rude

Snow Dream

i had a dream it snowed
finally
a big ass old school deep snow
i went out walking in it
wearing blue jeans no coat
deep snow up to my crotch
a guy all bundled up said
"it's gonna be cold
snow is gonna stay
all winter"
up to my crotch
okay
mmm
better make a
therapy appointment

I Define Me

i am a walker and a bicycle rider
i am a parent of two young children
i am a husband
i am a cis gendered queer white male
i am middle class
i am the proud son of a transgender veteran
i am a person who has failed and learned
i am a homeowner in a capitalist economy
i am a nurse, writer, artist
i am 30% Irish according to a genetic test
i am a survivor of abuse
i am happier now after doing personal therapy work
i am a rebel who dismantles the patriarchy
i am a rebel who feels like a failure for not doing more
i am fifty three years old
i am bald, fuck hair
i feel like a new poet
i feel like doing good things
i feel like somebody wants me to shut up
i am okay with that
i am out of here

Celebrate Our Universe

Hello Summer

Last night before reading
bedtime books
jabbed my finger into a unicorn
covered with sequins
one of them slid under my finger nail
screamed and began to bleed
my daughter was concerned
she touched the unicorn and said
look, it poked my finger too, see?
held her hand close to my face
hey, I think we stopped bleeding
everything is okay daughter
we will be okay
that's what you call a freak accident
now we know
move slowly around sequins.

In the morning walking to work I see
the deer slept in today
three heads peeking out of the grass
in the wild space out behind the alley
rain has risen the little green things like
a resonating note biological harmonics
lilacs bloom and invite themselves in
through open windows and into my mind
hello summer

Party With Sunspot AR3664 At The Jensens

Severe Geomagnetic Storm Watch
a thunderstorm also rolls through
drinking birthday whiskey in
single car stand alone garage
roll up door open
the first act is over
curtains of rain clear
intermission
clouds move away over this
freshwater inland sea then
green horizon and purple sky
vertical lines of color appear and vanish
swirls and spirals between us and the stars
our necks bent up
neighbors stop to look and talk
people we've never met
invisible cosmic structures now revealed
planetary shield illuminated
the electro magnetic field of home
resonating with our
pulsating electrical hearts

The Inter-Dimensional Pandemic Council Dream

I have a recurring dream that I've been asked to be on the Inter-Dimensional Pandemic Council and weird stuff starts happening like during the meeting we're talking about power and I looked out the window and saw a wooden crate appear on the shoreline of the river below the secret meeting warehouse and then out of that wooden crate two wolves run down the shore and i told them i saw this and they said that's really happening. Then i held up a paper with a zero with a line horizontally through it and that was our symbol it had power to rally us. Later I look it up and this circle with a vertical line is the 21st letter in the Greek alphabet meaning Phi used in physics with quantum mechanics and in math representing the Golden Ratio an irrational number approximately 1.618 (okay i am not a mathematician why am i on this council) Somehow these strange disruptions come from another dimension and they are sentient and aggressive and weird and psychedelic, and not the good kind of hallucinogens, and also they are pathogenic to humans.

    The council is composed of the most eclectic group of people which is how I end up on it because a wide range of people prevents it from being corrupted from the inter-dimensional pathogen entities that can focus on one type of person and disempower them but drastically different people have frequencies that are hard to find and infect.

To our awake conscious mind, a re-occurring dream like this seems so strange. Why do i need to go through multiple plays of this scenario? Think about it deeper, is life getting more stable, or is life getting weirder and not good weirder by the hour? Yes this whole scenario might be a metaphor for confronting the unknown, but it might not also be an actual vision of the future. Bring it on, we are ready. Organize Earth.

Message In A Canning Jar

Sunday night on the beach in darkness
a tiny wind pushes waves from the North
over mysterious waters
sand hard a little frozen the beach wilderness
lights of Duluth on far shore
responsible citizens tucked in bed
alarms set for Monday
beach silent and empty
strangely soothing darkness
rotating airport light at the end of the point
sweeps the sand with photons
confirming I am alone and have nothing to fear

Art Crawl In Space

poetry in space
engraved on the side of a craft
piloted by robotics
and slow signals from Earth
Who is our audience here?
some sentient life that
has already experienced
the Voyagers gold plated copper disks
(a double album released to space
way back in 1977)
the aliens are ready for the sequel.

if there are beings
out there in the cosmos
who desire the experience of exo-art
we are ready for them

>
> -inspired by Ada Limon's
> "In Praise Of Mystery: A Poem For Europa"
> launched on the NASA Europa Clipper mission
> to contemplate another water world
> in our solar system.

Maude Would Greet This Day With A Breath Of Fire

looking out the front window over the lake
our living room is the bridge of a ship
anchored to mother vessel planet Earth
every day turning toward the future
watch our star appear on the horizon
every day the blast of color at dawn
and shadows contrast the light we
welcome the blue skies dammit
i am going for a spacewalk
front door opens warm
the breath of life springs at me
each step each breath a new
realization
what have i been doing before this moment
no judgment
this is not the time
feel the fire now
without sunscreen without a hat
no protective clothing from solar radiation
just for a few minutes
while i enjoy being alive
standing outside our front door
in my underwear
greeting the dawn
with a breath of fire

Merry Solstice!

On Earth
in the Northern Hemisphere
the end of December
is a sacred time when
we welcome back the light
on the 21st of December
the nights grow shorter
and the days grow longer
we have decorated evergreen trees
to celebrate life in death
during the cold darkness winter
we have put a star
at the very top of our tree
to shine down life giving energy
a star that represents our star
The Sun
which is why
we are alive.

Listen When Body Speaks

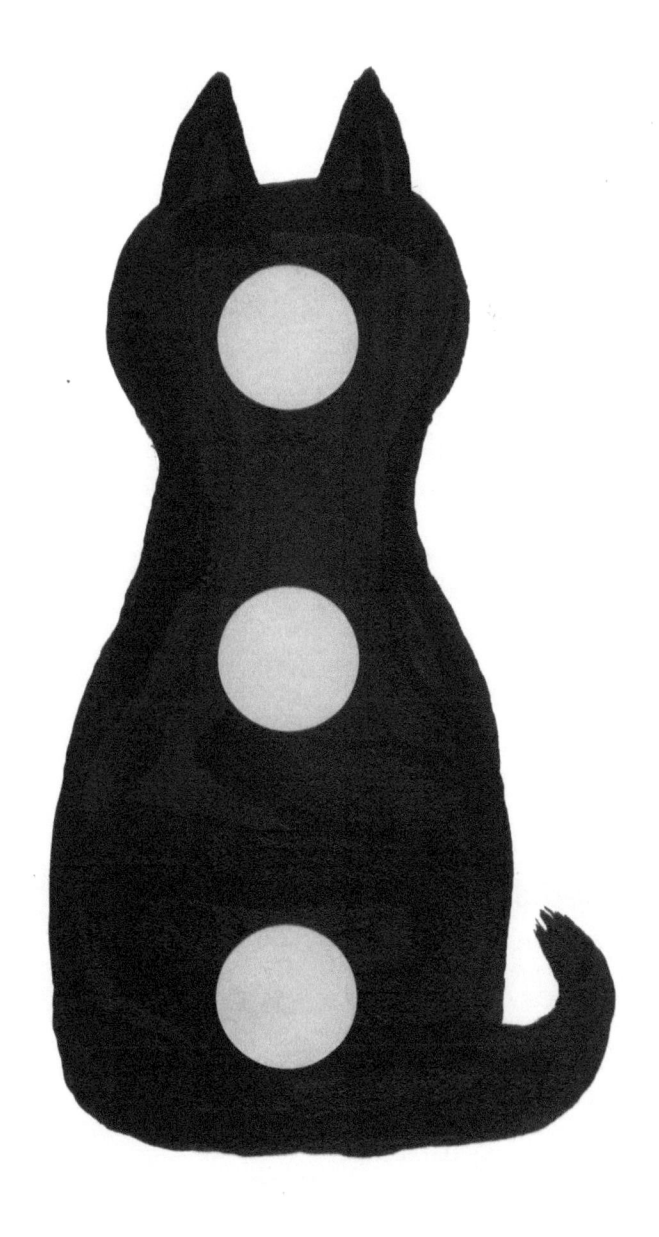

Love & Science

last night i absorbed my son's pain
breathing it in with every breath
laying next to him while going to sleep
our heads touching
he cried softly
body still covered in red rash
low fever from mystery virus
as i breathed in i
accepted his pain
breathing out i sent him
healing calming light
it gave me an instant headache
that grew worse with each breathing cycle
each mantra
(voice of fear says
this is really working
am i hurting myself
this is painful)
with each breath in
absorbing his pain
he quieted a little
and soon his breath
became slow and steady
his body calm and he slept
yes he also had real medicine
to relieve his symptoms

acetaminophen and topical analgesic
we do evidence based healthcare
the power of human touch is real
it's not magic not faith
there are things about the human body
we have barely begun to understand
the magnetic field of a human heart
can be felt by another human
three feet away
and even the touch of a hand that lasts five seconds
can communicate a bouquet of emotions
laying next to my child
my arms around him
our magnetic fields intertwined
resonating
breathing in we calm our bodies
breathing out we smile
transmission received
the power of love
does heal

Listen To Your Body

listen to your body
speaking in voices loud and quiet
when we wake in the morning
listen
as body wakes up there are
messages for us
what needs to change
what needs to continue
the voice may be hard to understand
maybe we need to ask for translation
someone who can interpret
what the body says
be brave and
ask for help
you can always
refuse advice
listen to your body
show your body some love
every day
every hour
let body stretch
let body look into the horizon
let body relax with it's feet up
let body eat good food and get enough sleep.
everyday is a gift
we must unwrap it

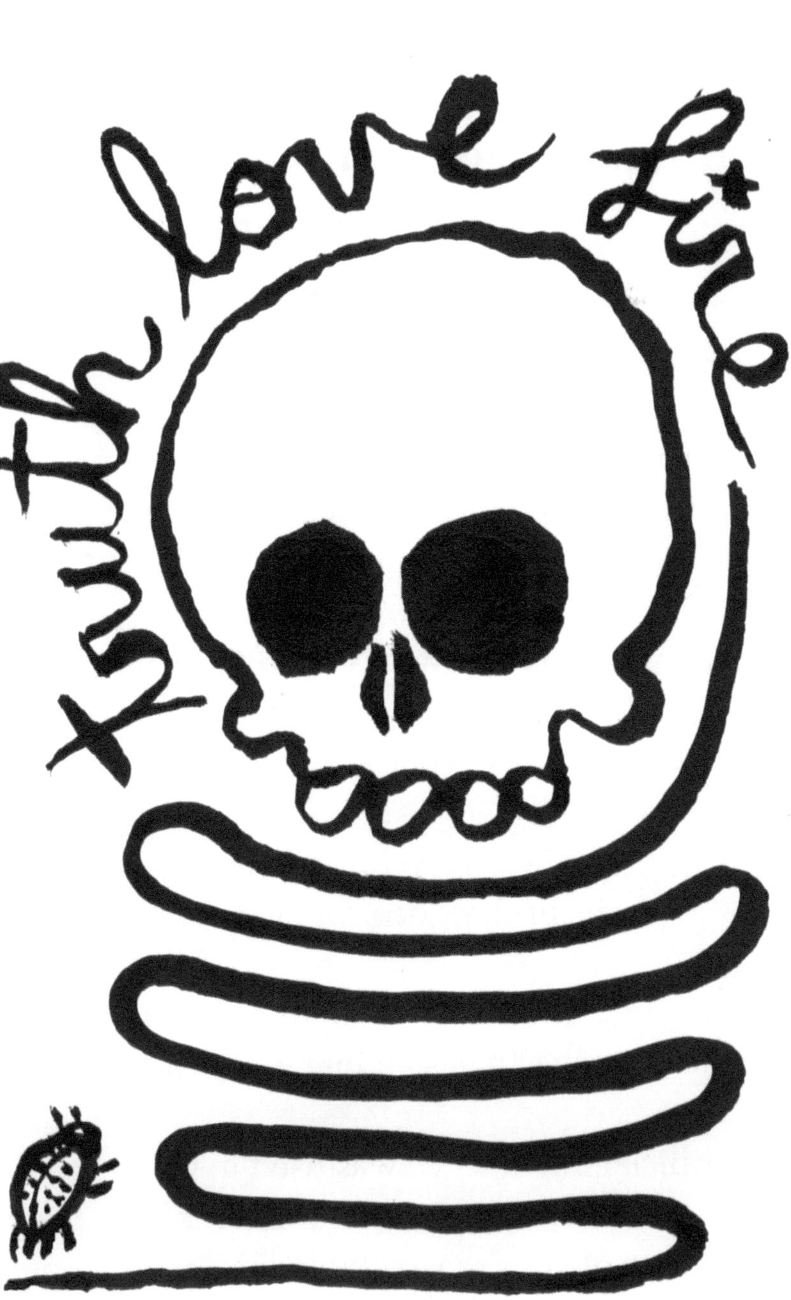
truth love line

Thank you to my first reader Sonja Wildwood for never ending love.

Thank you to the Duluth Poetry Chapter for enthusiasm and support. This book would not be here without you.

Thank you to Wussow's Concert Cafe and The Studio Cafe in Duluth, Minnesota. Both of these local shops are huge supporters of the arts and deserve our love.

Thank you to Jordan Sundberg at tincupdesignco.com for cover art.

The use of a lower case "i" in this book to indicate first person perspective is an intentional act of humility.

No artificial intelligence was used in the making of this book. (no offense to the newborn AI babies, we're just suspicious of your creepy billionaire parents, and does family therapy for AI even exist yet?)

If you found this book and want to reciprocate for this gift with a donation that will be saved to create and share another book, please use the Venmo below. Pay what you can, suggested price is $10. Thank you.

Venmo: @Robert-Wildwood

venmo

Reading

Volume 1: Peter Wohlleben *The Power Of Trees* / Daniel J. Siegel & Tina Payne Bryson *The Whole Brain Child* / Linda LeGarde Grover *The Sky Watched* / Jess Morgan *Too Many Hats* / Jan Chronister *Decennia* / Bell Hooks *All About Love* / Emily August *The Punishments Must Be A School*

Volume 2: *Climate Grief: From Coping to Resilience and Action* by Shawna Weaver, *The Hidden Staircase* by Carolyn Keene, *Morphology* by Anastasia Bradford, *It's All Too Much I'm Ready To Become A Canada Goose* by Henry Kneiszel, *Onigamiising: Seasons of an Ojibwe Year* by Linda LeGarde Grover, *Dead Dad Jokes* by Ollie Schminkey.

Listening

Volume 1: M0 *Kindness* / Gryffin *Whole Heart* / M0 & Gryffin *Reckless* / Danny Go *Ice King* / Idina Mensel *Let It Go* / Jawbreaker *Busy* / Celtic Women *Putomayo Music* / Varttina *Soleniko* / Beyonce *Renaissance* / Shankar Vedantam *Hidden Brain Podcast* / Brene Brown *On Blame*

Volume 2: More of Shankar Vedantam *Hidden Brain Podcast*, LoFi Hip Hop Radio - Beats to Relax/Study To (no words, good for writing!), woodpeckers in the woods, children singing, wind through the trees.

Robert Wildwood does creative writing, public art projects, and performances while working as a nurse and raising two children with his partner in Duluth. Wildwood serves as Secretary in the Duluth Poetry Chapter of the League of Minnesota Poets.

Wildwood has been published by Microcosm Publishing, The Nemadji Review, The Thunderbird Review, Duluth Superior Pride Zine, New Verse News, Agates, & The Journal of Undiscovered Poets. Wildwood published his first book of poetry Hillside Sunrise in 2022 followed by Like A Leaf Love The Sun in 2023 and Sun Ripened Fun Ideas: V1 in 2024.

* *Wake As Water* and *Solidarity* first appeared in *The Thunderbird Review*.
* *Enjoy Primitive Recreation, Big To-Do List, Password: Henry Loves The Snow, & Play Until You Die* first appeared in *The Nemadji Review*.
* *Apply Pressure, No Peeking* first appeared in Agates 90th anniversary special edition.
* *When Everything Is Here* first appeared in The *Journal of Undiscovered Poets*.

@robertwildwood.bsky.social
RobertEarlWildwood.wordpress.com
RobertEarlWildwood@gmail.com

Portrait of Robert Wildwood

by Beatrix Wildwood (Age 5)